Noggin and the Dragon

For Katy

Noggin and the Dragon

by Oliver Postgate and Peter Firmin

KAYE & WARD
194–200 BISHOPSGATE
LONDON E.C.2

First published as a hardback by
EDMUND WARD (PUBLISHERS) LTD
1966
Reprinted by
KAYE & WARD LTD
1972
First published in paperback 1972

ISBN 0 7182 0232 5 (hardback)
ISBN 0 7182 0361 5 (paperback)

All inquiries and requests relevant to this title should be sent to the publisher, Kaye & Ward Ltd, in the City of London, and not to the printer.

Printed in England by Jarrold & Sons Limited, Norwich

This is the castle of Noggin the Nog.
Noggin the Nog lived here
a long time ago.

Noggin the Nog was in his castle.
Nooka was with him.
Nooka was his queen.

Little Knut was Noggin's son.
He was in the castle
with some of his friends.
They had come to speak to Noggin.

Knut said:

'My friends and I want to go on a hunt.
We want to go to Dragon Valley
and hunt a dragon.'

Nooka did not like this. She said:
'They are too small to hunt dragons.
They are only boys.'
Noggin smiled and said to her softly:
'Do not worry.
There are no dragons in Dragon Valley.
The dragons went away a long time ago.

Noggin spoke to the boys.

'Here is my battle banner,' he said.

'Take it with you to Dragon Valley.

If a dragon sees you he will know that you are my friends and he will not harm you.

'But if you find a dragon
you must not chase him or stick
swords and spears into him.
You must greet him as my friend.
Offer him sweets if you have any.

‘Thor Nogson will go with you.
Thor Nogson is a brave soldier.
Thor Nogson will look after you.
Go with him now. He will give you
all the things you need
to take with you.’

Thor Nogson gave each boy a blanket.
He gave each boy a little shield and sword
and a shiny hat to keep off the rain.

He took two candle lamps
and a big tin of sweets.

They set off from Noggin's castle.

They walked proudly.
They carried the banner
high in the air.

They walked up the hills.

They walked over the mountains.

They came to Dragon Valley.

There all the plants and trees are very big,
very much bigger than the plants
in other places.

They hunted for dragons
among the huge plants.

They climbed the huge trees.
They hunted through the caves.

They did not find any dragons.

Soon it was time for bed.
Little Knut and his friends
found sticks and branches
for a fire.

Thor Nogson lit the candle lamps.

Little Knut and his friends curled up in their blankets and slept by the fire.

Thor Nogson sat on a rock
and watched over them.
Thor Nogson was not afraid of dragons.

In Dragon Valley
everybody was asleep.

The birds in the
huge flowers slept.

The little animals slept.

Soon Thor Nogson slept too.

Late that night a storm came up.

The thunder roared.
The lightning flashed.
The wind blew the cold rain
across the rocks.

The rain ran down Thor Nogson's nose.

He woke up.

He looked up.

He saw a strange beast with flaming eyes.
'EEK!' he cried. 'A dragon!'

Thor Nogson jumped up.
He ran round the rock.

The dragon ran after him.
As it ran it made a noise.
A noise like many small voices crying
'Wait for me! Wait for me!'

Thor Nogson saw that the fire was out.
Knut and the boys were not there,
but the dragon was there.

Thor Nogson ran away.

He ran as fast as he could
down the mountain side.

The dragon ran after him.
'Wait for me! Wait for me!'
it cried as it ran.

Thor Nogson beat on
the door of Noggin's castle.
'Let me in! Let me in!
A huge dragon with fiery eyes
is chasing me!'

The soldiers took
bows and arrows.
They ran to
the castle walls.

Soon the dragon came down the hill.

'Open the door,' said Noggin.

The dragon was six wet little boys.
Its fiery eyes were two candle lamps.

'Why did you boys pretend to be a dragon?'
said Noggin to Little Knut.
'You were very naughty.
You frightened poor Thor Nogson!'
Little Knut said:
'We did not pretend to be a dragon.
We held up the big leaves to keep
the rain off.
We held on to each other in a line
so that we would not get lost.
We came to tell Thor Nogson
that we wanted to go home,
but he ran away!'
Queen Nooka said: 'No more talking.
The boys are tired and cold and hungry.'

Noggin made up the big fire in
the great hall of the castle.
Nooka made hot soup for the dragon hunters.
They drank it all up
and soon they fell asleep.

the end